HOT D

Written by Nora Gaydos
Illustrated by BB Sams

innovativeKids®

A dog.

A hot dog.

A hot, hot dog.

A hot dog got on a log.

A hot dog got on a log
in the fog.

A hot dog got lost on a log.

A hot dog got lost on a log
in the fog.

SOB! SOB!

Stop the log!

A hot dog flops off the log.

After You Read

Answer these questions about the story, and then use words from the story in fun, new ways!

1. What is the dog riding on?
   Why does the dog get lost?

2. What other words rhyme with *dog*?
   What other words rhyme with *hot*?
   What other words rhyme with *sob*?

3. Make up a different sentence of your very own for each of these words: *lost, fog, stop.*
   Now try to use all of those words together in *one* sentence!

Skills in This Story

Vowel sound: short *o*
Sight words: *a, on, in, the*
Word ending: *-s*
Initial consonant blends: *st, fl*
Final consonant blend: *-st*

FROG COPS

Written by Nora Gaydos
Illustrated by BB Sams

The frog.

The frog with spots.

The frog with spots robs.

The frog with spots
robs the shop.

The frog with spots
robs the mop shop.

The frog with spots
robs the mop shop
by the pond.

KNOCK, KNOCK!

The frog with spots
drops the mops.

The frog cops trot
in the shop.

The frog cops lock up
the frog with spots.

After You Read

Answer these questions about the story, and then use words from the story in fun, new ways!

1. What kind of shop does the frog rob?
    Why does the frog drop the mops?

2. What other words rhyme with *shop*?
    What other words rhyme with *lock*?
    What other words rhyme with *trot*?

3. Make up a different sentence of your very own for each of these words: *frog, pond, cop*.
    Now try to use all of those words together in *one* sentence!

Skills in This Story

Vowel sound: short *o*
Sight words: *the, with, by, in, up*
Word ending: *-s*
Initial consonant blends: *fr, sp, dr, tr*
Final consonant blend: *-nd*
Initial consonant digraph: *sh*